IMAGES
of America

THE INLAND
WATER ROUTE

THE BEGINNING OF THE INLAND WATER ROUTE. The Inland Route in Northern Michigan is a navigable series of lakes and rivers stretching from Cheboygan in the east to Conway in the west, with the end of the route formerly linked by a brief train ride to Petoskey. The Cheboygan Crib Light, this small but important beacon in Lake Huron, would have marked the very beginning of the route for those who began their trip in Cheboygan. (Author's collection.)

ON THE COVER: INLAND ROUTE DOCKS. Here at the Liebner-Davis docks at Cheboygan, passengers arrive by stagecoach to begin their journey on Northern Michigan's Inland Water Route (See page 21). (Inland Water Route Historical Society.)

IMAGES
of America

THE INLAND
WATER ROUTE

Matthew J. Friday

ARCADIA
PUBLISHING

Published by Arcadia Publishing
Charleston SC, Chicago IL, Portsmouth NH, San Francisco CA

Printed in the United States of America

Library of Congress Control Number: 2009943860

For all general information contact Arcadia Publishing at:
Telephone 843-853-2070
Fax 843-853-0044
E-mail sales@arcadiapublishing.com
For customer service and orders:
Toll-Free 1-888-313-2665

Visit us on the Internet at www.arcadiapublishing.com

To Homer and Octavia Friday

CONTENTS

ACKNOWLEDGMENTS

Completing a work of this size is no small task, and yet again I am deeply indebted to those who have helped me along the way. Help came in so many different ways, from loaning pictures to include in this book to helpful words of encouragement from friends and coworkers; every gesture is something I am deeply grateful for.

The Inland Water Route Historical Society in Alanson has been of tremendous assistance while putting this project together. The images and historical information they have provided will assure future generations that the history of the Inland Route and its communities will be preserved. The work they have done and continue to do is worthy of the highest commendation.

The Historical Society of Cheboygan County has also been extremely helpful by providing images and historical documents that have been used extensively throughout this work. The same can be said of the Little Traverse Regional Historical Society in Petoskey, which provided some incredible images that are included here. I am also especially grateful to Doug Dailey, who has been kind enough to allow me to include many images from his collection in this work.

Other words of thanks are due to the Clarke Historical Library at Central Michigan University, as well as the Cheboygan and Mackinaw Area Public Libraries.

To my family and friends, I cannot thank you enough for your encouragement and support during the various stages of writing this book. Your help is essential to the completion of such a task, and without it I would lose what is probably the greatest of all motivators.

Finally, I wish to thank you, the reader. I have done my very best in compiling this book, which is not just a pictorial history of the Inland Route, but a book that tells its story as well. I hope that as you journey on the Inland Route you come to know a bit more of the history of Northern Michigan and realize just how diverse and dynamic it is.

INTRODUCTION

Northern Michigan's place as a vacation destination is nothing new. Now in its third century, tourism in the north has become a part of what makes up the identity of the northern portions of the Lower Peninsula. From tourism's earliest days right up to the present, the Great Lakes have provided much of the attraction. But inland there are yet more waters to traverse—the majestic Inland Route.

The Inland Route (sometimes referred to as the Inland Waterway), a series of interconnected lakes and rivers from the city of Cheboygan in the north to the village of Conway in the south, offers some of the most majestic and beautiful scenery in all of Michigan. The entire trip, one way, is about 43 miles. From north to south, the route touches the communities of Cheboygan, Mullett Lake, Aloha, Topinabee, Indian River, Alanson, Ponshewaing, Oden, and Conway. In days past, passengers aboard the Inland Route steamers could disembark at Conway or Oden and take a train into Bay View or Petoskey. Numerous other smaller named settlements also exist in places along the route, though they may only consist of a few cottages.

But it would be remiss to only acknowledge the Inland Route as a tourist attraction. Long before any European set foot in the area, the northern waterways were used by the area's Chippewa (Ojibwa) and Ottawa (Adawe) Indians, both for transportation and trade. Parts of the route were narrow or shallow, but this proved to be less of a problem for canoes than it would for steamships in the future. Native Americans used the Inland Route for trade with each other, as well as seasonal migration. Any number of encampments existed along the way, many of which have today been researched and documented. The Cheboygan River, Mullett Lake, Burt Lake, and Crooked Lake all had sizeable Native American settlements.

Then, as now, each part of the Inland Route offered something different. From the cold depths of Mullett Lake to the meandering and twisting of the aptly named Crooked River, not only was the scenery something to behold, but the very water beneath the traveler was as well. But the Inland Route was not merely a natural wonder to be enjoyed; it had a much more important utilitarian use.

With the arrival of Europeans beginning in the 17th century, the "tip of the mitt" area took on new importance for both its strategic location and its role in trade. The trade in animal pelts—fur—created the first major economic boom in the north. Fort Michilimackinac and later Fort Mackinac both played pivotal roles for the trade in furs to be shipped back to insatiable European markets. Essential to gathering furs were those who penetrated the rivers and lakes of the area, setting traps and trading with the Native Americans. The waters of what today make up the Inland Route no doubt played an important role. Not only could traders penetrate the interior region, it also made travel around Waugoshance Point unnecessary. Waugoshance, on the far northwest corner of the Lower Peninsula, was a treacherous point to try to travel by small craft such as a canoe. As there was frequent interaction between Native Americans on the western side of the state and those to the north and east, traveling around Waugoshance Point was a considerable danger. Bypassing it through use of the Inland Route no doubt saved countless lives. Indeed, the First Peoples are to be thanked for truly utilizing what would become known as the Inland Route.

The mouth of the Cheboygan River was of particular importance to the Inland Route, as historical records indicate its role as a meeting place with the area's Native Americans and the British and French from the forts. As early as 1776, fur trader John Askin owned a small house on the river, and there was likely at this time a small settlement of traders, Native Americans, and even a couple of slaves. But the name "Cheboygan" also refers to the river's limited role: the name probably comes from the Annishinaabe *zhiibaa'onan*, meaning a channel or passage for a canoe. At the time, it was not navigable for much more than that.

At any rate, the fur trade lasted until the mid–19th century, at which time the declining availability of fur and decreasing demand threatened to wipe out commerce in the area. Fishing became a viable industry for some, and the U.S. Army base at Fort Mackinac maintained its strategic importance, but these would not be enough to keep the north growing.

Northern Michigan had been blessed by an abundance of white pine. As the United States expanded westward, the lumber available here was necessary in building a nation. There was a voracious demand for timber, and due to the abundance of it in the north and the excellent shipping avenues (being surrounded by two Great Lakes), Northern Michigan was in a naturally advantageous position. The first lumber mill was set up in Cheboygan in 1844 by Alexander McLeod, who had moved there from Mackinac Island. The next year, his employee Jacob Sammons built the first permanent residence in town. Many others soon followed, and Cheboygan and its nearby sister city of Duncan City both grew quickly. By the 1880s, both had become important lumbering communities.

On the western end of what would be the Inland Route, settlement began at Petoskey just a few years after it had begun at Cheboygan. Though it had long been a substantial Native American settlement, white missionaries began moving into the area in the early 1850s. A Reverend Dougherty had been performing missionary work there for some time, but it was not until 1852 that Andrew Porter, a Presbyterian missionary, arrived with his family and began long-term work in the area. It would take seven more years before anyone would arrive with business interests. In 1859, Hazen Ingalls came to the area and purchased a sawmill formerly belonging to Harvey Porter, Andrew's brother. He also operated a small store for the local Native Americans and the Porters. Early settlement here was not as rapid as it had been in Cheboygan and Duncan City, but the Bear River was nevertheless soon realized as an important source of power for sawmills. The small settlement, once dubbed Bear River, was renamed Petoskey in 1873 in honor of Native American chief Ignatius Pet-o-sega. Like Cheboygan and Duncan City, Petoskey also flourished as a lumbering town.

But in order for these towns to prosper as they did, many changes had to be made to the natural surroundings. For the Inland Route, much work had to be done to the waterway to make it more navigable. Once this was done, booms of logs could be floated downriver to the mills, and ships carrying supplies could be sent upriver. The earliest improvement took place in 1846, when Alexander McLeod and his brother Ronald constructed a dam at the Cheboygan rapids to utilize the power the rushing water could provide for their sawmill. In 1867, the Cheboygan Slack Water Navigation Company was organized with the purpose of improving the river. By 1869, a canal and lock had been completed at the rapids, making easier travel up and down the river a reality. In the early 1870s, the first of many dredging projects had been completed, making it possible for larger vessels to sail the river. There can be little doubt that as a result of these early improvements, further interest was fueled in the Cheboygan settlement.

More improvements were made in the 1870s at about the middle of the Inland Route. In 1874, Francis M. Sammons removed an obtrusive sandbar at the mouth of the Indian River as it spilled into Burt Lake. State funds helped provide additional resources to construct piers at the point to prevent the sandbar from reappearing. In 1877, the Sturgeon River, which once flowed into the

Indian River, was rerouted to flow directly into Burt Lake and thus prevent the buildup of more sandbars. Thus the Inland Route had been cleared and made truly navigable. The primary purpose of all this was to connect Cheboygan and Petoskey to facilitate the efficient transportation of mail. Until the arrival of the railroad a few years later, mail was hauled by boat from Cheboygan to the west end of Crooked Lake and then by stagecoach to Petoskey.

While the Inland Route would always be important to the lumber industry, as railroads began encroaching into the area in the 1880s, rail took on a larger role. Spur lines off railroad tracks often brought felled lumber directly to mills instead of having to float it downriver. As rail traffic increased, however, so did the number of those seeking to escape to the solace of the north. This meant a new identity not just for the big lumbering towns—namely Cheboygan and Petoskey—but also for the smaller lumbering towns that had popped up along the Inland Route, such as Indian River and Alanson.

With the increased tourism, new communities sprang up along the Inland Route that, more or less, existed only for tourism and relaxation. Topinabee and Aloha are but two examples of communities that had hotels, cottages, and certain entertainment outlets, but little more—although that was the idea. The purpose of living or vacationing along the Inland Route was to get away from the busy world and enjoy peace and solitude at its finest.

By the 1880s, the Inland Route had become a popular vacation destination. Those coming from far away would either arrive by rail or by one of the many lake steamers that would dock at the McArthur Dock in Cheboygan. The Detroit and Cleveland Navigation Company (and others) would bring their large vessels into Cheboygan and Petoskey on frequent, regular schedules. About a mile south of the mouth of the Cheboygan River, steamships would be loaded up and passengers would sail through the waterway, occasionally stopping off for an hour, a day, or a week. The steamers made regular, scheduled trips and passengers could disembark at their leisure. Many chose to spend a few days traveling the route, perhaps spending a night at the Hotel Topinabee, and another at the Buckeye House, before completing the journey in Oden. From there a short train ride would take voyagers to Bay View and Petoskey. Others chose to make the entire journey, and back, in a day. Some also chose to expand their journey by taking an Arnold Line or Island Transportation Company boat from Cheboygan to either Bois Blanc or Mackinac Island.

Hotels along the Inland Route were more like resorts. Most offered social activities, such as dancing, and all offered fine meals and the opportunity to interact with other travelers. In the small communities along the route, vacationers could enjoy ice cream, bowling, and billiards, among other activities. The goal of a trip on the Inland Route was relaxation, and proprietors of shops and hotels along the way saw to it that no expense was spared in taking care of their guests. To quote one contemporary source, a promotional booklet called *Where to Spend the Summer: Michigan Resorts on Little Traverse Bay*, "No one should miss a day on the beautiful Inland Route, which includes numerous silver lakes and winding rivers, alive with game fish. The passing of numerous little crafts under sail and steam, the swiftly moving panorama of limpid waters and verdant shores, form a most effective panorama of scenic grandeur."

The vessels that meandered through the lakes and rivers of the Inland Route were either owned by companies specifically organized for the purpose of moving guests along the water or by the owners of some of the larger hotels. Examples include the Inland Navigation Company, New Inland Route, and the Liebner-Davis Line to name a few. Some of these vessels would even have their own band playing onboard for the pleasure of their guests.

The Inland Route continued to be a popular vacation destination until the mid-1920s. With the decline of lumbering and migration of populations from the north, the Inland Route lost the large vessels plying along the water. Many of the hotels stayed open, however, and some would continue to do so for the next several decades. Individuals, too, chose to navigate the Inland Route. As the steamers gradually disappeared, more and more boaters took to the route themselves. Boat races and regattas occurred with considerable frequency, and the Inland Route is still home to the Top-O-Michigan outboard races.

Today the Inland Route remains heavily traveled by pleasure seekers, albeit in a different way than 100 years ago. Still, it attracts people from all over the country to explore Northern Michigan at its finest and most picturesque. The Inland Route has changed, but its role as a voyage for recreation and relaxation has not.

A description from 100 years ago is just as pertinent today as it was then. Again, from *Where to Spend the Summer: Michigan Resorts on Little Traverse Bay*, "The Inland Route is not only one of Northern Michigan's greatest attractions, but it is one of the most picturesque, and the only boat trip of its kind to be found on the American continent. Go where you will, wander where you may, you will find nothing that surpasses the scenic grandeur of this chain of lakes and rivers." If the past is any indication of the future, things are not likely to change anytime soon.

One

SETTING SAIL

CHEBOYGAN CRIB LIGHT. If one image could symbolize the beginning of the Inland Route, the Cheboygan Crib Light might be it. Marking the dredged entrance into the Cheboygan River from Lake Huron, this light safely guided mariners into the river to dock at the bustling city. Originally constructed in 1884, this rare image shows the crib in its original place. Since relocated to the shore, it still marks the beginning of the river. (Author's collection.)

ARRIVAL AT THE MCARTHUR DOCK, C. 1915. Many vacationers choosing to take a voyage on the Inland Route arrived here at the McArthur Dock near the mouth of the Cheboygan River. Originally owned by the W. and A. McArthur Company, it was later purchased by Millard D. Olds, a prominent Cheboygan lumber baron, whose piles of lumber can be seen in the background. Ships from the Detroit and Cleveland Navigation Company and Arnold Line docked here regularly, and from this spot they sailed to places all across the Great Lakes. Here the *City of Cleveland III* makes her way into Cheboygan. Launched in 1907, she prowled the Great Lakes until 1950 when she was severely damaged in a collision and eventually sold for scrap. (Above, Doug Dailey; below, author's collection.)

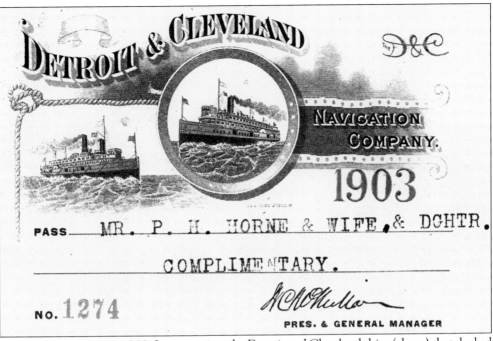

SHIP PASSES, 1902 AND 1903. It was not just the Detroit and Cleveland ships (above) that docked at the McArthur Dock, but also those of the Arnold Transit Company (below.) While Arnold Line ships no longer dock in Cheboygan, the company, formed in 1878, still operates passenger and freight vessels to Mackinac Island from their docks in Mackinaw City and St. Ignace. The bearer of these passes, Phillip H. Horne, was the manager of the McArthur Dock for some 25 years until his death in 1907. He came to the city in the 1870s, when Cheboygan was just beginning its real growth. In the *Cheboygan Democrat*, he was described as "a quiet unassuming gentleman, who never made an enemy, and those most intimately connected with him in his work are most enthusiastic in their praise of the man." (Both Historical Society of Cheboygan County, Inc.)

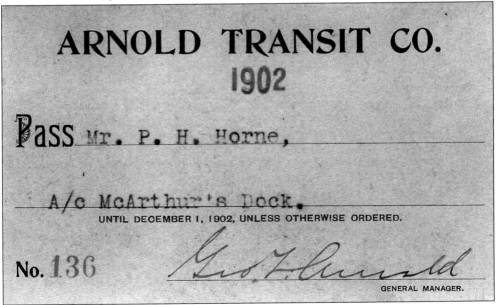

MICHIGAN CENTRAL DEPOT, 1918. Water was by no means the only way to reach Cheboygan and begin a trip on the Inland Route. Located just adjacent to the McArthur Dock was the Michigan Central Railroad depot, seen here. The railroad arrived in Cheboygan in 1881, providing a much needed regular connection to the remote north. Prior to this, seasonal navigation provided the only real regular link to places further south. (Author's collection.)

DETROIT AND MACKINAC DEPOT. The Detroit and Mackinac Railway challenged the Michigan Central's hegemony in Cheboygan beginning in 1904. Like most railroads, it published literature inviting people to take their trains to new places. This included the D&M's Mackinac Route, which brought travelers to Cheboygan, and from there invited them to join an excursion on the Inland Route. (Author's collection.)

THE NEW CHEBOYGAN HOTEL, C. 1910. Before embarking on a trip through Northern Michigan, travelers would frequently spend a few days in the bustling city of Cheboygan. Those seeking the best in accommodations would often stay at the New Cheboygan, built in 1884. It was initially called the Michigan Exchange, and later it operated as an annex of another nearby hotel, the Ottawa. (Author's collection.)

THE GRAND CENTRAL HOTEL, C. 1890. The Grand Central Hotel was located about midtown and offered travelers a place to stay right on Main Street. This photograph shows one of Cheboygan's short-lived horse-drawn streetcars, which linked Cheboygan with nearby Duncan City. Hotels and amenities offered in Cheboygan explain why it was called the "hub city of the resort region." (Author's collection.)

DOWNTOWN CHEBOYGAN. Not only was Cheboygan the hub city of the resort region, but it was also the hub city for regional business. Its position on the river no doubt helped it grow into the region's center for professional services and banking, as evidenced by the majestic First National Bank building (above, left.) Cheboygan's population peaked near 9,000 in the mid-1890s and then rapidly fell as the lumber boom ended and the mills that employed so many closed and took the workers with them. The river, which made Cheboygan, thankfully had another industry—tourism. For those who came north on vacation, many chose to see that river firsthand by traveling the Inland Route. (Above, Doug Dailey; below, Historical Society of Cheboygan County, Inc.)

CHEBOYGAN COUNTY COURTHOUSE, C. 1910. Cheboygan is the county seat of Cheboygan County, and its government was located here in this building—probably the most photographed building in the county's history. Completed in 1900 at a cost of $35,000, it was replaced by a new county building in 1969, and soon after this building was sadly demolished. (Author's collection.)

M. D. OLDS MILL. Cheboygan's best-known lumber baron was Millard D. Olds, who operated this mill from about 1904 to 1916. Located across the river from the McArthur Dock, Olds was a resourceful man who made money any way he could, even when most lumber mills had already closed. Today the Coast Guard cutter *Mackinaw* moors at the site of this mill. (Author's collection.)

THE CONGESTED CHEBOYGAN RIVER. It is easy to see from this photograph why Inland Route boats that left from Cheboygan usually did so from farther up the river. This image shows just how congested it could be, with logs being floated to mills and schooners waiting to haul lumber away. Scenes such as this were typical for much of the history of the area, as log booms could appear at just about anyplace along the Inland Route. (Doug Dailey.)

TUG ON THE CHEBOYGAN RIVER, 1908. Not all of the boats in the Cheboygan River or even the Inland Route were passenger vessels. Tugboats were also essential to moving log booms and helping larger ships navigate as well as assisting with dredging operations. In fact it was a tugboat, the *Maud S.*, which was the first vessel to traverse the entire Inland Route. (Author's collection.)

THE CHEBOYGAN SWING BRIDGE. This iconic piece of Cheboygan's history was the first bridge one encountered when traveling up the Cheboygan River. Constructed in 1877 at a cost of $6,500, the swing bridge rotated on a center pivot to allow vessels to pass by on either side. Passing children were often happy to offer their assistance in turning the center-mounted windlass to swing the bridge. (Doug Dailey.)

LINCOLN AVENUE BRIDGES. The second major bridge one encountered on the Inland Route is the span at Lincoln Avenue. Four bridges have crossed the river here; the John F. Bridge (pictured) was condemned in 1973 and replaced by an entirely new structure a few years later. That bridge was replaced with an impressive new span in 2007. (Author's collection.)

EMBARKING FOR THE INLAND ROUTE. Although not all trips on the Inland Route began from Cheboygan, regularly schedule departures from Cheboygan usually left from this dock that was operated by the Liebner-Davis Line of Cheboygan. Here the *Ida L II* takes on passengers and prepares for departure up the river and onto the inland lakes and rivers. In the background are the Lincoln Avenue Bridge and the Union Bag and Paper Company. Though this dock is gone today, there are still remnants of the pilings in the river—a silent witness to the thousands of people who once passed over this dock. (Inland Water Route Historical Society.)

U.S. 27 AND U.S. 23 AT LINCOLN AVENUE. Probably taken about three decades after the images on pages 20 and 21, the same approximate location had changed considerably; a new bridge, and the Inland Route boats were no longer docking near the grocery store seen in this image (center left). (Doug Dailey.)

LOOKING SOUTH FROM LINCOLN AVENUE. Looking upriver from near the location of where the Inland Route dock once was, one can see that as soon as the ships would have left the dock passengers were in for a peaceful and pleasant ride out of town as they made their way along the river. (Doug Dailey.)

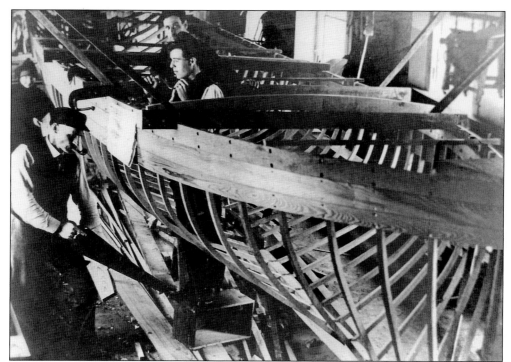

THE *IDA L.* UNDER CONSTRUCTION. One of the best known Inland Route lines was the Liebner-Davis Line, headquartered in Cheboygan. First operating in 1909, the company was organized by August Liebner and his son Ernest. Purchasing a boat kit by mail, they constructed what was later christened the *Ida L.*, seen here as it is being assembled. Along with Charles Davis of Alanson, who operated the *Tourister II*, the Liebner-Davis Line was the first boat company that took passengers the entire length of the Inland Route. The Liebners were bold by going into business when they did, as Cheboygan's population was beginning its rapid decline after the lumber boom. However, they were quite timely as tourism was the up-and-coming industry, and their venture would soon prove lucrative. The *Ida L.* was named after August's daughter Ida. (Historical Society of Cheboygan County, Inc.)

LAUNCH OF THE *IDA L.* The *Ida L.* was launched on June 5, 1909, in the Cheboygan River, shown here at the very moment it began plying the Inland Route. The Liebner-Davis Line was met with immediate success, and soon a newer, larger vessel would be operating for the company: the *Ida L. II.* (Doug Dailey.)

THE *IDA L. II* IN THE CHEBOYGAN RIVER LOCKS. In order for any vessel to get from the mouth of the river to places further up, a passage through the river locks is required. Completed in 1869 at a cost of approximately $30,000, the completion of the lock was one of the great facilitators of growth in Cheboygan. Without it, the growth of the area's industry would not have been possible. (Doug Dailey.)

VESSELS IN THE CHEBOYGAN RIVER. Early travel along the Inland Route was usually done by larger ships such as the *Ida L. II*. But as more and more people owned their own vessels, travelers increasingly plied the route (or a portion of it) themselves in private boats such as those shown above. The river, however, remained an important stopping-off point for vessels too large to sail the Inland Route, such as the sailboat shown below. Due to bridge heights and the limited size of locks along the way, these vessels could only travel part of the length of the Cheboygan River. Though the styles of boats have changed, scenes such as these are still common in the river today. (Both author's collection.)

YACHT GADABOUT ON THE RIVER. Pleasure boats such as the *Gadabout* were not an uncommon sight on the Cheboygan River or the Inland Route. Here the ship is weighed down with those seeking the calm and relaxation of a pleasant cruise on the river. The American Bag and Paper Company can be seen in the background. (Doug Dailey.)

WEST SIDE OF THE CHEBOYGAN RIVER. When looking at an image such as this, it is difficult to believe that at one time the river was hardly passable for canoes. But the Cheboygan River has undergone numerous dredging and widening projects over the years, making it truly possible to realize its wealth as the gateway to the inland seas. This view of the river shows numerous pleasure boats docked along its west side. (Doug Dailey.)

SPIES COMFY CABINS, CHEBOYGAN. Due to its natural beauty, it is no surprise that numerous motels and cabins sprouted up along the Inland Route through the years. Spies Comfy Cabins catered to both boaters and motorists with their ideal location downtown. Rooms were outfitted with Rittenhouse furniture, which today is highly collectible. Though the cabins are no longer standing, a motel continues to operate on the site. (Doug Dailey.)

THE CHEBOYGAN RIVER IN WINTER. Once the cold winter months set in, there is no travel by boats on the Inland Route; the entire length often freezes completely over. It still sees plenty of use, however, by ice fishermen who drag shanties directly onto the ice and fish through holes bored into it. Some places along the Inland Route, such as Mullett and Burt Lakes, freeze so much that vehicles can be driven onto the ice. (Doug Dailey.)

AIRIAL VIEW OF CHEBOYGAN
Looking down the River.   © J.R. Johnson. #64

CHEBOYGAN BY AIR, C. 1940. The sprawling city of Cheboygan can be seen here as it envelops the area around the Cheboygan River. At the mouth there is evidence of abandoned docks where lumber schooners once called. In the middle of the photograph is the old Swing Bridge (see page 19). This image shows just how important the river was to Cheboygan's development and the significant role that it played then and continues to assume in the area's survival. It is interesting to note how few trees are visible in this image. When the lumber industry faded, others rose to the occasion, including tourism, which has become the north's most important means of employment and business. While the lumber mills of old have long since passed, the river continues to act as an industrial and recreational artery for the city. (Doug Dailey.)

Two

MULLETT LAKE

MULLETT LAKE VIEW. One of the greatest expanses on the Inland Route, Mullett Lake features unrivaled importance in the history of Northern Michigan. From its early role as a gathering place for local Native Americans to the lumber boom and tourists and settlements that followed, Mullett Lake has seen its fair share of changes over the years. Named after surveyor John Mullett, the lake that bears his name is a fitting legacy to the great importance of what he first surveyed from 1840 to 1843. (Doug Dailey.)

THE HACK-MA-TACK INN. At the very spot where the Cheboygan River empties into Mullett Lake, the Hack-Ma-Tack Inn, originally constructed as a private hunting and fishing lodge in 1894, continues to serve guests with impeccable service and the finest meals. Guests would know when lunch was served through the ringing of a bell from the bell tower. Bands also frequently played at the inn, sometimes alternating among different stops along the Inland Route. Most of the original structure burned and was rebuilt in 1925, but through the years the Hack-Ma-Tack has provided a stop for travelers along the Inland Route from the days of the small steamers to today's pleasure boats. (Both author's collection.)

THE CHEBOYGAN RIVER AND MULLETT LAKE. This image, taken from the Hack-Ma-Tack, shows the Cheboygan River as it empties into Mullett Lake (left). It is at this point that Inland Route travelers voyaging from Cheboygan got their first look at one of the great inland seas along the route. This particular area was also known for its excellent fishing. (Author's collection.)

THE WALDEMERE CLUB AT DODGE'S POINT. After the Hack-Ma-Tack, the next stop on the Inland Route was the Waldemere Club, located on Dodge's Point. It was first opened in 1893 as a private, exclusive club for the area's elite. An astounding $15,000 was spent on its construction. Association members purchased individual lots nearby for building their own cottages while taking meals and enjoying entertainment at the clubhouse. (Historical Society of Cheboygan County, Inc.)

THE HOTEL WALDEMERE. By about 1905, the Waldemere Club had changed from a private club to a public hotel. This allowed for private citizens, such as those traveling along the Inland Route, to stop for a room or a bite to eat. The hotel featured 17 rooms and a dining room that seated 100 people. The hotel rarely made money, however, and was torn down in the mid-1920s. (Doug Dailey.)

PINE GROVE HOTEL, C. 1910. Originally built by George J. Dodge in 1883, the Pine Grove Hotel was at first nothing more than Dodge's home; but beginning in 1885, he and his wife started serving meals to local mill workers. By 1903, an addition had been built and the Dodge residence had become a bona fide hotel. Herbert and Sarah (Dodge) Parks later took ownership of the hotel, and Herbert would frequently entertain guests in the evening by telling stories in the lobby. Sunday chicken dinners at the Pine Grove were renowned, and reservations had to be made each week for those wishing to partake. Guests, both visitors and locals, waited on the porch until Mrs. Parks rang the dinner bell, after which they entered and took their seats. Waiting on the table was stewed chicken, homemade dumplings, biscuits, and vegetables. Ice cream and homemade pies followed for dessert. After decades of catering to Inland Route guests and locals, the Pine Grove Hotel was torn down in 1956. (Author's collection.)

MULLETT LAKE ROAD, C. 1920. By the 1920s, area roads were improving enough so that vehicular traffic became more frequent—and practicable. Residents of Mullett Lake could then either drive into Cheboygan or take a short train ride to the city for shopping and socialization. Mullett Lake Village was an important stop on the Inland Route that catered to tourists, but in time it became a more permanent residential community. (Doug Dailey.)

ROBERTS'S STORE AND POST OFFICE, C. 1937. Some shopping could be done locally, however, rather than going to Cheboygan. The Mullett Lake Store, seen here, was purchased in 1917 by Bill and Edith Roberts. The store also served as the village's post office; note the P.O. boxes visible in the background. Standing from left to right are Erma Roberts, Norma Roberts, and postmistress Virginia Baier Roberts. This store closed in 1958. (Historical Society of Cheboygan County, Inc.)

GEORGE OBENAUF. A native of Chicago, George Obenauf came to Mullett Lake in 1910 and soon built a modest boat factory and storage facility on the shores of the lake. Here he manufactured wooden boats, affectionately known as "Obie Boats." After making them here, he sold them throughout Northern Michigan. Obenauf was very particular about his work and insisted that each piece of seasoned lumber that went into his boats was perfect. In the image above, Obenauf is seen hard at work constructing a boat. Below, he tries one out on the water. He continued to build boats until shortly before his death in 1958. (Both Historical Society of Cheboygan County, Inc.)

THE OBIE BOAT. Most of George Obenauf's carefully constructed boats were clinker built (lapstrake) and made in 12-, 14-, and 16-foot lengths. He also made a child's pram eight feet in length that could be used as a dinghy. A meticulous craftsman, Obenauf carefully selected not only the wood for his boats but also hired good craftsmen to make sure his vessels were of the finest quality. Obenauf usually used cedar for his boats, but at least one example survives that is made of cypress and not lapped. This boat has been restored and is accessible to the public for viewing at the Cheboygan County Museum. Obenauf was not particularly interested in boat motors, so he hired 20-year-old Hobart Kirsch in 1924 to assist him in this part of the business. Kirsch ended up purchasing his boss's marina in 1938. Many of Obenauf's original buildings still stand on the site that is now Hobart's Marine. (Historical Society of Cheboygan County, Inc.)

BIRCHWOOD (SILVER BEACH). When railroad traffic first came to the area in 1881, the Michigan Central Railroad ran along the western shore of Mullett Lake. Though not a regular stop for Inland Route steamers, the whistle-stop community of Birchwood, later called Silver Beach, was one of many the lake steamers would have passed and occasionally disembarked at, with rail travelers utilizing this miniscule station. (Author's collection.)

THE SILVER LODGE. The Silver Lodge, located at Birchwood/Silver Beach, catered to the needs of motorists by offering cabins and amenities for those traveling along the lake by road. Many of the original buildings still exist, and the area is now a private resort community at a pristine location. (Doug Dailey.)

Long Point. A small point jetting into Mullett Lake marks the location of Long Point, another small community of cottages that dotted the lake's shoreline. Most of the cottages were simple affairs, as can be seen in this humble Long Point abode. Larger than Birchwood, Inland Route vessels would occasionally stop here. (Author's collection.)

Long Point Depot. Small railroad depots dotted the entire length of Northern Michigan railroads, which made travel to Inland Route locations also possible by rail. This was a welcome luxury for those living outside the major cities and villages, as the countryside remained relatively isolated until improved highways were constructed in the 1920s. (Author's collection.)

MIAMI BEACH. Though developed later, Miami Beach was another small hamlet located along Mullett Lake, located just north of the village of Topinabee. Inland Route steamers did not dock here, but after the dawn of the age of the automobile motoring along the lake became popular along what is currently U.S. 27. Like Silver Beach, Miami Beach offered travelers a place to stay, fuel up, and grab a bite to eat. Some of these structures are still standing in various states of repair. Miami Beach is also at the east end of Mullett-Burt Road, which connects directly to Burt Lake to the west. The location of Miami Beach is also near the former site of the tiny community of Bushville, an African American settlement that existed in the early history of the county. (Both Doug Dailey.)

THE DOCK AT ALOHA. Nearly directly across from Long Point on the opposite side of Mullett Lake is the village of Aloha. A popular stop for Inland Route steamers, the dock seen here was constructed by the Detroit and Mackinac Railroad in 1911. It was originally 300 feet long and three feet wide; from here, passengers could disembark their boat and meander into the village. (Doug Dailey.)

BOATS AT ALOHA. Aloha was then and is now a popular spot for boating, fishing, swimming, and camping. The village popped up around a sawmill and store shortly before the Detroit and Mackinac Railroad came through in 1903. The railroad knew that Aloha could be a popular resort destination and soon began advertising it as such. The availability of the Inland Route boats made it all the more desirable. (Doug Dailey.)

ALOHA RAILROAD STATION. Betting on Aloha becoming a popular destination, the Detroit and Mackinac built this elaborate railroad station around 1904 at an unimaginable cost of $14,000. With a log cabin–themed interior and exterior, fieldstone fireplace, and large benches cut out from a single log, the depot was as elegant as they came for Northern Michigan stations. It was built primarily out of bird's-eye maple, an extremely rare wood prized for its beauty. The main part of the station housed the waiting area, ticket office, and telegraph office; a smaller building housed items waiting to be shipped, including luggage. The depot continued to serve the community until the 1940s, and the larger portion of it was torn down in 1947. The smaller building that remained operated as the Aloha House of Gifts, but it was torn down in the 1960s. (Both Doug Dailey.)

MAIN STREET, ALOHA. This early image of Aloha, probably dating around 1905, shows the Susie Stinchfield house, later called the Luke Cross Hotel (far left), general store (left), and the Detroit and Mackinac stationmaster's house (right). With the addition of the train station, these few buildings made up essentially the entire village in the early 1900s. (Doug Dailey.)

ALOHA STORE AND STATIONMASTER'S HOUSE. The Aloha Store seen here (left) was first constructed by Fred Haut to cater to homesteaders in the area and also functioned as the post office until 1915. In that year, stationmaster Henry Harsh was awarded the job of postmaster and converted one bedroom in his house (right) to be the village post office, where it remained until 1924. From 1924 to 1942, the post office reverted back to the original Aloha Store building. (Doug Dailey.)

Aloha Bathhouse. Aloha had several bathhouses over the years, and this one is likely the largest of them. Bathhouses usually offered saunas and a relaxing environment for patrons, and they were always divided by gender. In 1911, the Detroit and Mackinac Railroad built a bathhouse for ladies at Aloha, measuring 12 feet by 14 feet, which "will prove very convenient to those desiring to enjoy the lake bathing at this pleasant little resort," the *Cheboygan Democrat* reported. (Doug Dailey.)

Bathing at Aloha. The beach at Aloha has for generations been a place for relaxation. In this image, several small boats are visible along the shore, and what is probably a bathhouse can be seen to the left. Though the attire worn while at the beach has changed considerably from the time this image was taken, probably around 1915, the beach is still used for swimming and recreation. (Historical Society of Cheboygan County, Inc.)

DETROIT AND MACKINAC RAILROAD PARK. Between the depot and Mullett Lake, the railroad owned eight acres of land that were used as a park. This land also provided a beach for those who traveled in by rail or Inland Route steamers to use for recreation and relaxation. This land was eventually abandoned by the railroad, but it would soon see new use. (Doug Dailey.)

ALOHA STATE PARK. With the goal of creating a state park, the eight abandoned acres of railroad property were purchased by Cheboygan County. An additional 20 acres of adjoining vacant land was purchased to bring the total acreage to 28—the smallest amount the state would consider for making a park. Thus, in 1923, the Aloha State Park was born. (Doug Dailey.)

The Aloha Dock, c. 1935. Though the dock at Aloha State Park no longer received guests on Inland Route vessels, the park continued to be popular among those traveling by automobile. The building seen here at the end of the dock was the park's caretaker's quarters, registration building, and bathhouse. It was completed in 1929. (Doug Dailey.)

Dr. James Patterson Farm. The land on which the village of Aloha is situated was owned by James Patterson, who had inherited substantial holdings from his father Robert. Robert cut trees on his property at a mill he had constructed on the lake. James later divided the land between the platted village (in 1903) and his extensive farm seen here. (Historical Society of Cheboygan County, Inc.)

PIKE'S SUMMER TAVERN. Crossing Mullett Lake back to its west side, voyagers on the Inland Route arrived at Topinabee. H. H. Pike, following the progress of the Michigan Central Railroad as it headed north in 1881, purchased a piece of land along the lake (through which the railroad would run) and platted it as the village of Topinabee. He opened the hotel seen here in 1882 to cater to vacationers heading north. However, the village took on an even more important role once voyages on the Inland Route became popular beginning in the 1890s. Those on day trips usually took lunch in Topinabee, with the ships *Northern Belle*, *Topinabee*, *Ida L.*, and *Ida L. II* making frequent stops. Pike's Summer Tavern burned in 1917 but was soon replaced by the Hotel Topinabee. (Doug Dailey.)

TOPINABEE RAILROAD STATION, 1918. H. H. Pike was rewarded for his forward thinking the year after he bought the land that would become Topinabee, when the Michigan Central came right through his lakefront property. A railroad depot was soon built, and the small village that sprouted up became accessible by boat or rail. This depot still stands today, though the railroad is gone. (Author's collection.)

SCENERY AT TOPINABEE. The village of Topinabee is situated directly on the shores of Mullett Lake, and the railroad passed close along its shore. A boathouse and small dock can be seen in this c. 1910 photograph. The village is named after the powerful Potawatomi chief Topinabee (or Topenebee), whose name translates to "Quiet Sitting Bear" or "Peacemaker." (Doug Dailey.)

THE STEAMER TOPINABEE. Of all the vessels to ply the Inland Route, the largest and most elaborate was the steamer *Topinabee*. She was built in 1899 in Charlevoix, Michigan, by the Beauvals' Ship Yards at a cost of $5,000 to $6,000. The *Topinabee* was 64.9 feet long, 14.5 feet wide, had a depth of 2.5 feet, and weighed 16 gross tons. She had a wood hull and a top speed of 12 to 14 miles per hour via her twin, three-foot-diameter screw propellers. Passengers were treated to numerous comforts, including upholstered seats, brass trimmings, a carpeted deck, an onboard orchestra, and even a toilet room. In the cabin, office, pilothouse, and upper works, polished quarter-sawed Ohio white oak added an ornate touch. The *Topinabee* usually met up with other Inland Route vessels at Topinabee, from where she would carry passengers further up the route until the final destination at Oden or Conway. (Inland Water Route Historical Society.)

THE TOPINABEE UNDERWAY. The *Topinabee* was licensed to carry a maximum of 250 passengers. In case of inclement weather, she had retractable canvas sheets that could be dropped down to "house in" the lower deck. She was also equipped with a telescoping funnel and hinged pilothouse so that she could clear low bridges. Officers, crew, and the orchestra all wore uniforms. The ship called at the dock at Pikes Summer Tavern, which was also used by other Inland Route boats. Renamed the *Pe-To-Se-Ga* in 1911, the vessel meandered along the Inland Route until about 1920, when its homeport was changed from Petoskey to Grand Haven, Michigan, and later to Erie, Pennsylvania. She was rebuilt twice, in 1911 and 1917, and was abandoned because of age in 1926. (Inland Water Route Historical Society.)

THE HOTEL TOPINABEE. After Pike's Summer Tavern was destroyed by fire in 1917, the Hotel Topinabee, which replaced it, was even more magnificent than its predecessor. Seen here, the Hotel Topinabee had 67 sleeping rooms and a magnificent porch facing the lake with plenty of docks for Inland Route voyagers. (Doug Dailey.)

RUINS OF THE HOTEL TOPINABEE. Unfortunately the Hotel Topinabee suffered the same fate as the hotel that it replaced—twice. Under the new name, the hotel was destroyed by fire in 1928. It was rebuilt following nearly the exact same design as the one that was burned. This image shows just how thorough the fire was in consuming the magnificent structure. (Doug Dailey.)

HOTEL TOPINABEE IN LATER YEARS. After its reconstruction in 1928, the Hotel Topinabee continued to serve guests along the Inland Route. Unfortunately the Great Depression soon followed, along with decreasing traffic along the route, which plunged the hotel into dire financial straits. The hotel was sold to Edward Moloney Sr. in 1935 for $850, and again it became profitable, operating until 1950. Falling into disrepair it burned yet again in 1965 and soon after what was left was removed. Boat races along the Inland Route frequently began here at the Hotel Topinabee. In 1910, the Topinabee Yacht Club held their first regatta in 1910. The *Cheboygan Democrat* reported, "The race there will be worthwhile, knowing the character and standing of the men at the head of the club of that place." All were invited to participate and "the outsiders are most urgently invited to come and enjoy the sport with the Topinabee sportsmen. . . . The day is going to be a big red-letter event for the resorters, boatmen, and all that enjoy this class of good, clean sport." (Author's collection.)

STORE AND POST OFFICE, C. 1910. Topinabee was a resort community, but the provisions of daily life were still necessary. There were few stores in the community, but H. G. Vorge was happy to supply these goods. Next to it was the Topinabee Post Office (left). Topinabee's first post office was established in 1882 at the same time that the small village was just being born. (Doug Dailey.)

MAIN STREET, TOPINABEE. The main street through Topinabee made it easy for motorists to join Inland Route travelers, as the road went directly by the Hotel Topinabee (center, seen through the trees). The railroad tracks and train station were also just off this street. Topinabee's advantage was that it was accessible by boat, train, or automobile. (Doug Dailey.)

MAIN STREET (U.S. 27), c. 1955. Topinabee continues to be a resort community to this day, though many of the houses there are now occupied year-round. The majestic hotels are gone, and the main street through town, U.S. 27, looks nearly identical to this image taken in the mid-1950s. Over the years, Topinabee has had everything from restaurants to orchards (owned by Charles Parrish) to bakeries (operated by Irene Train) to a hardware and sporting goods store (seen here at left) owned by Marvin Hood. Topinabee was also known for its natural spring water, sold under the label Sanitas Springs. Bottled in special heavy, clear-glass bottles imported from Austria, this water was served both in Topinabee and on Michigan Central trains. Despite its small size, Topinabee has had an important place in the history of Northern Michigan and the Inland Route. (Doug Dailey.)

Three

INDIAN RIVER
AND BURT LAKE

VILLAGE OF INDIAN RIVER. Flowing from Mullett Lake, the Indian River makes a brief journey until it reaches the end of its trip into Burt Lake. On the shore of Burt Lake, the village of Indian River lies along the river of the same name, with the Sturgeon River also passing through. The village has had a history of industry and tourism—much of it attributable to the Inland Route. (Historical Society of Cheboygan County, Inc.)

INDIAN RIVER, C. 1890. The location upon which the village of Indian River sits was an ideal spot for a settlement. Situated where the Indian and Sturgeon Rivers and Burt Lake all meet, it was perfect not only for business, but recreation as well. In this image, a variety of private and Inland Route boats can be seen docked along the Indian River. (Inland Water Route Historical Society.)

NEAR THE MOUTH OF THE INDIAN RIVER. Originally the Sturgeon River emptied into the Indian River just before the latter in turn emptied into Burt Lake. Because a sandbar quickly formed in the Indian River from the inflow, the Sturgeon was diverted in 1877 at a cost of $9,939.50. This change made the Inland Route much friendlier to navigation. (Doug Dailey.)

THE STEAMSHIP *DUQUESNE*, C. 1884. An early Inland Route steamship, the *Duquesne*, is seen here in the Indian River. Operated by Frank M. Joslin, the ship is probably about the average size of steamers of this era. Later Inland Route vessels would be considerably larger. Joslin operated at least two other Inland Route ships, the *Pastime* and the *Oden*. (Inland Water Route Historical Society.)

THE STEAMBOAT *PASTIME*, C. 1884. Early on, Inland Route vessels had to deal with considerable challenges on the voyage, not the least of which were log booms floating down the rivers to area lumber mills. The *Cheboygan Democrat* prematurely opined in 1888 that the Inland Route was essentially a "thing of the past" due to prevalent river obstructions. (Inland Water Route Historical Society.)

THE *IDA L.* AT INDIAN RIVER. Tourism on the Inland Route began in earnest in the early 1880s, though the late 1870s did see some travelers on the route as well. The most well known of the early lines was the New Inland Route Line, which probably operated until about 1900. The Liebner-Davis Line was the last of the regular lines to ply the route, and their *Ida L.* can be seen in these photographs taken on August 22, 1909. The images are possibly from the first trip the *Ida L.* took, with 54 passengers aboard. She can be seen above docked at Indian River at Martin's Dock, where Inland Route ships usually tied up. Behind her is the *Tourist*. Below she is making her way out of the Indian River and into Burt Lake. (Both author's collection.)

THE STEAMER ODEN AT INDIAN RIVER. The *Oden* enjoyed a long and celebrated career on the Inland Route. Built in 1890 and owned by Frank Joslin, she was originally a tugboat, but 20 feet were added to her center three years later and she became an Inland Route steamer. She docked at all major locations along the route, from her main port of Oden all the way to Cheboygan (see page 91). (Inland Water Route Historical Society.)

THE RAMBLER, C. 1909. Smaller vessels such as the *Rambler* were much easier to navigate along the Inland Route due to the seemingly ever-present challenges of other vessels, log booms, and sharp curves in the river. The *Rambler* is seen here docked at Indian River about 1909. The man with his foot on the boat is Roy Stokan. (Author's collection.)

INDIAN RIVER, C. 1885. Indian River's pioneers believed that the railroad would one day pass through the area. Like H. H. Pike in Topinabee, their inklings proved correct. F. E. Marin of St. Louis, Missouri, built a store in 1879 and relocated here permanently in 1881. A post office was established in 1879 in the back of Martin's store, with Oliver S. Heyden as the first postmaster. A second store followed, then—perhaps not surprisingly for a boomtown—a saloon was opened. Most of the early buildings were quickly constructed wood-frame structures, as can be seen here. The McHenry House can be seen in the image below, later renamed the Alcove Hotel. Note the dirt streets in both images. (Both Historical Society of Cheboygan County, Inc.)

LOOKING WEST ON RIVER STREET. The original 1879 F. E. Martin store can be seen in this image (far right), here occupied by J. W. Lester's grocery store. Immediately to the left is the new store and post office, constructed in 1898. A dock was also built from the back of the new store directly to the Indian River behind it. To the left of the post office is McHenry's Variety Store. (Doug Dailey.)

RIVER STREET, c. 1940. Decades later, the scene on River Street had changed little. The buildings described above were all still standing, and even the post office was situated in the same building. A massive fire in 1911 destroyed much of the village, but these historical structures were spared from the conflagration. (Doug Dailey.)

INDIAN RIVER DEPOT, C. 1910. Indian River was also easily accessible by railroad after the Michigan Central first came into town in 1881. The railroad is part of the reason why Indian River was settled at all; in 1876, John B. Clark, David Smith, Jackson Corey, S. P. Hayes, and M. A. McHenry all moved to what would become Indian River, hoping the railroad would some day come too. Thankfully they were right. The fountain seen here was installed in 1900. (Doug Dailey.)

INDIAN RIVER BRIDGES, C. 1903. At right can be seen the main bridge across the Indian River. The road going over the bridge is Sturgeon Street (today U.S. 27); most of the buildings in this image were destroyed in the 1911 fire. The railroad bridge at left is the second one at the site and is seen here after it was installed in 1903 by the Michigan Central. (Doug Dailey.)

The New Bridge, Indian River, Mich.

CAMELBACK BRIDGE, 1924. This new bridge was constructed across the Indian River in 1924 and built by the J. B. Whitcomb Construction Company. Called "camelback" bridges for their appearance, bridges of this design are technically known as concrete curved chord through girder bridges. An extremely rare design, this type of bridge was only built in Michigan and Ontario and usually only in rural areas. They were designed for simplicity in construction as well as safety, with little maintenance required. The bridge is 91 feet long and has a roadway width of just 22 feet—making crossing it when opposing traffic is present a bit of a harrowing experience. Camelbacks were usually always narrow, at least by modern standards. Original sidewalks can also be found on the camelback bridge, also uncommon for this design. (Doug Dailey.)

TUSCACRORA TOWN HALL. In many rural communities, the township hall served as an important gathering place for meetings, elections, entertainment, and celebrations. Indian River is located in Tuscacrora Township, and the hall above, constructed in 1902, was in many ways the center of the community. Stage shows were presented here as well as some very early silent films. One of the signs on the building advises passersby that there is "dancing after the shows." Although it escaped the 1911 fire that destroyed much of the village, the original wooden structure was consumed by fire in the early 1920s and replaced by the structure seen below in 1924. (Above, Doug Dailey; below, Historical Society of Cheboygan County, Inc.)

THE PINEHURST INN. A popular destination on the west side of town, the Pinehurst Inn was ideally situated to accommodate passing boaters as well as motorists. Traveling along the Inland Route, it would have been among the first buildings people saw as they came into the village. It is still standing today, though it is no longer the impressive resort seen here. (Doug Dailey.)

Burt Lake Golf Club, Indian River, Mich.

BURT LAKE GOLF CLUB, C. 1925.
Although Inland Route traffic decreased in the late 1910s, Indian River enjoyed a considerable flow of vacationers traveling in on the highway. Burt Lake Golf Course was built in 1922 just outside of town and attracted a great deal of those seeking outdoor recreation. Today the course is known as the Indian River Golf Club. (Doug Dailey.)

BUTTERFLY FALLS
INDIAN RIVER, MICH.

BUTTERFLY FALLS, INDIAN RIVER.
Indian River was known to be a prolific source of natural spring water. One account described, "Of late the inhabitants have procured a flowing well wherever they have gone deep enough. The pressure of these wells is about 16 pounds to the square inch. Good water for man and beast is the best medicine, and tourists have derived great benefit from the waters of this village." The best-known spring waters in the county flowed at Butterfly Falls and the Michigan Central Railroad depot fountain. (Doug Dailey.)

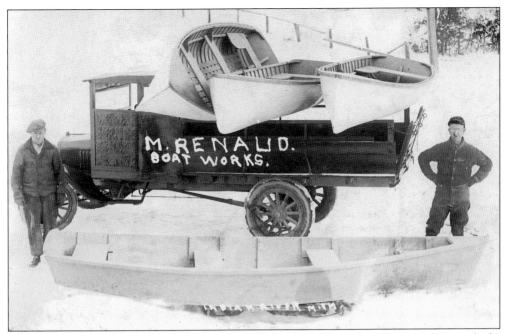

INDIAN RIVERBOAT WORKS. Many individuals along the Inland Route had their own boat works for the obvious reason of their proximity to the water. Indian River had at least two: the M. Renaud Boat Works (above) and H. T. Dagwell's. Despite these photographs, Renaud is a bit of a mystery. Dagwell was better known, though his worldwide renown may have been a bit exaggerated in this 1898 description from the *Cheboygan, Up-to-Date*, "[He] has worked up a world-wide reputation by the fine boats he puts up. He is situated at the bend of the river, where he has every advantage of location. He superintends his own work and so thoroughly is it done that as a consequence he ships boats to the south, the east, the west, and the north." (Both author's collection.)

U.S. 27 THROUGH THE YEARS. These images, taken from nearly the same location but roughly four decades apart, show a stretch of U.S. 27 as it passes through town. The large house on the left in the image above is the former home of state senator Calvin A. Campbell. A former railway conductor and manufacturer, Campbell served in the senate from 1927 until he died in office in 1933. Though originally an Inland Route destination, Indian River continued to do well with the advent of vehicular traffic. In the image below, the street has swelled to include numerous restaurants and three gas stations within two blocks. (Both Doug Dailey.)

LOOKING NORTH, U.S. 27. The main street through town in the 1930s shows King's Restaurant, O. H. Garby and Sons' Garage, and the A&P grocery store. Signs advertise fishing tackle, Mobilgas, and Arctic Ice Cream. Today this street still holds numerous restaurants and shops catering to tourists and locals alike. (Doug Dailey.)

MCCLUTCHEY'S AND DOWNTOWN, C. 1940. One of Indian River's longtime downtown fixtures is McClutchey's clothing store. Opened in June 1936 by Sam and Donna Bess McClutchey, the business remains in the family to this day. The Indian River Inn next to it offered guests the luxuries of private bathrooms and steam heat. (Doug Dailey.)

RIVER AND HIGHWAY, C. 1940. By the mid-1920s, Inland Route traffic through Indian River had all but ceased as far as the large passenger vessels were concerned. Private craft then plied the waves much more frequently. However, Indian River would draw its fair share of motorists as well. Because two highways passed through it, the small village was in a fortuitous location. But what really changed Indian River was the coming of Interstate 75 (I-75). In 1960, a portion of the highway was completed from Indian River north to Topinabee; in 1962, the segment from Gaylord up to Indian River was completed. The fact that I-75 was so close made it easy for motorists to stop off and make a stop here. I-75 changed many of the communities it passed through, providing a much-needed influx of traffic into towns that might otherwise struggle to exist. Indian River had come a long way from its simple beginnings as an Inland Route destination. (Doug Dailey.)

Park Tavern on Burt Lake, Indian River, Mich.

VIEW OF BURT LAKE. The second lake one enters on the Inland Route is Burt Lake. It is named after William Austin Burt, who, along with John Mullett, first surveyed the lake from 1840 to 1843. This image is taken from the shore of Park Tavern, formerly known as the Argonaut Club, also known as Pittsburgh Landing or Pittsburgh Resort. The Argonaut Club was formed about 1894 and was a private club located just west of the mouth of the Indian River. One description from the *Cheboygan, Up-to-Date* painted the location as a "natural paradise" and claimed, "Any agreeable person who is lucky enough to know some member or officer, can secure accommodations through such member or officer, and the privileges are such as money will not buy elsewhere." Numerous cottages also surrounded the clubhouse. Later the Argonaut Club was sold and became the Knights of Pythian Recreation Center. (Author's collection.)

BURT LAKE SCENIC TOWER. Located in Indian River, the Burt Lake Scenic Tower offered visitors a view overlooking the river and lake. The upper observation deck was equipped with a telescope, while an enclosed lower level provided views behind glass. The top deck was later covered and lights were added. William Austin Burt, the lake's namesake, discovered vast iron ore deposits in the Upper Peninsula and invented a typographer and solar compass. (Author's collection.)

VIEW FROM THE BURT LAKE SCENIC TOWER, c. 1933. This view from the top of the tower looks northeast. Mullett Lake can be seen in the distance. One account from the late–19th century *The Traverse Region, Historical and Descriptive, Illustrated* described, "No flies bother you as up in Canada, no 'skeeters nor any no-see-ums, nothing to mar the pleasures, no hot, stifling nights, no clammy dews, no dark miasma creeping into the system—but rest—sweet sleep at night and a dreamy existence by day." The area swelled with summer guests due to accounts such as this, often published in promotional material to draw new visitors. (Author's collection.)

THE TOURIST ON BURT LAKE. The *Tourist* navigated Burt Lake and Crooked River probably exclusively, rather than traveling the entire Inland Route like some vessels did. She operated in the first decade of the 20th century before being replaced by the *Tourist II* in about 1912. Her twin-screw propulsion can be seen in this unusual image along with her wooden rudder. (Little Traverse Historical Society Collections.)

THE TOURIST UNDERWAY. Packed with Inland Route travelers, the *Tourist* boasts lounge chairs on the upper bow. Other vessels serving the Burt Lake area included the *Rapid Transit* and the *Cygnet*, the latter owned and operated by C. W. McConnell. (Little Traverse Historical Society Collections.)

THE *TOURIST II* ON BURT LAKE. The *Tourist II*, along with the *Tourist* that preceded her, operated on Burt Lake and ferried guests between Sager's Resort, Pittsburg Landing, the Buckeye House, and Columbus Beach. Both vessels were powered by naphtha-burning engines. Popular around the turn of the century, naphtha engines were the preferred choice for small craft because of their reliability, safety, and ease of use. Boats on the Inland Route were generally steamships until the advent of naphtha engines, followed around 1920 by standard gasoline. Burt Lake lacked the number of towns and villages that Mullett Lake enjoyed, but those traveling the Inland Route frequently docked at the smaller resorts along the lake. Traffic typically stayed mostly to the south of the lake as the Indian River entered from the southeast corner and the next leg of the journey, the Crooked River, begins at about the center of the western shore. (Inland Water Route Historical Society.)

THE BUCKEYE HOUSE. The Edwin H. Sager family was one of the first to settle along Burt Lake; Sager came to Petoskey from Trumbull County, Ohio, walked to the lake, and soon purchased 64 acres of land. He returned to Ohio to gather up his family and built a log cabin in early 1879. In August of that year, he built the first frame house in the township at what came to be known as Sager's Landing. At the time, there were only three other white families living on the west side of the lake. Soon the home was expanded and it became Sager's Resort, and later it was renamed the Buckeye House. This first structure is seen in this early image. One newspaper account described the place by stating, "Sager's Resort is one of the most beautiful spots on Burt Lake for a summer home." In later years, a regular guest was former vice president Charles W. Fairbanks, who served under the Theodore Roosevelt administration. (Little Traverse Historical Society Collections.)

LATER BUCKEYE HOUSE. The Buckeye House was in many ways the center of the small community of Burt Lake. Originally known as Sager's Landing, the Buckeye House was one of the most popular destinations on the Inland Route. The hotel's meals were very well regarded, with both hotel guests and locals taking their meals there. Many of the settlers in the area were from the "Buckeye State" of Ohio, hence the name. (Historical Society of Cheboygan County, Inc.)

BURT LAKE POST OFFICE. The Burt Lake Post Office was established in 1878, but eventually the office was moved inside the Buckeye House, as seen here. The Burt Lake settlement was started by Edwin Sager and other early pioneers and soon grew to include the post office, general store, other cottages, and the Buckeye House. The hotel had three stories and 25 rooms. The Buckeye House burned in 1924. (Historical Society of Cheboygan County, Inc.)

BUCKEYE HOUSE IN FLAMES. By the time the Buckeye House burned in 1924, the era of the Inland Route steamers had come and gone. Edwin Sager's proud endeavors went up in flames—his original frame house and the hotel additions consumed in the conflagration. Wood-frame hotels were banned in later years in places such as Petoskey, and with good reason, as they had a tendency to burn. Once places like the Buckeye House caught fire, the flames spread rapidly. But unlike in the region's larger settlements, when Inland Route hotels burned, they were rarely rebuilt. As the area's boom period from the lumber era came and went, combined with decreased Inland Route traffic, there was little need for the places of lodging that once so frequently decorated the landscape. Many of the cottages that sprang up around these hotels, however, remain virtually unchanged to this day. (Historical Society of Cheboygan County, Inc.)

No. 5. Colonial Hotel, Burt Lake, Mich.

THE COLONIAL HOTEL. Of all the events in the history of Northern Michigan, one of the most controversial was near the site of the Colonial Hotel. A Native American community living near here, on Indian (or Colonial) Point, was burned out and evicted in October 1900 after a dispute over land ownership. The peninsula sticks out into Burt Lake from the western shore. The hotel seen above was built in 1895. Local Native Americans often sold handmade goods to voyagers on the Inland Route, especially to those who stayed here at the Colonial Hotel. In an ironic twist of fate, the hotel itself burned in 1909, the ruins of which can be seen below. A camp for girls was later established on the site. (Both Historical Society of Cheboygan County, Inc.)

RUINS, COLONIAL HOTEL, BURT LAKE, MICH.

Columbus Beach, Indian River, Mich.

COLUMBUS BEACH. Situated just north of Indian River, the Columbus Beach area was home to the large clubhouse seen here as well as many cottages located nearby. Davis Smith owned a small cabin at this site called Huckleberry Hall, but owing to an increasing number of guests from the Columbus, Ohio, region, the area promptly earned the name Columbus Beach. Two associations were formed near the site: the Central Ohio Tourists' Association in 1888 and the Indianola Summer Resort Subdivision in 1890. The two associations merged a few years later and used the clubhouse seen here. A casino and boathouse with 12 stalls and a common room above were added a few years later. The association also owned two boats—the *Columbus Maid* and the *Buckeye Belle*—which took association members to Indian River every day for shopping or other activities. Though on the Inland Route, it would not have been a regular stopping-off point for passenger vessels passing through the area. The Columbus Beach Club still exists today. (Author's collection.)

Four

CROOKED LAKE AND PETOSKEY

MOUTH OF THE CROOKED RIVER AT BURT LAKE. From the westernmost point of Burt Lake, the Inland Route continues into the Crooked River and ultimately into Crooked Lake. These bodies of water have appropriately earned their names, as they differ considerably from the significantly easier to navigate Cheboygan and Indian Rivers and Mullett and Burt Lakes. The Inland Route ends at the far end of Crooked Lake, just a few miles from Petoskey. (Author's collection.)

THE CROOKED RIVER. The Crooked River presents a considerable challenge to mariners even today, but for those who had to captain larger Inland Route vessels it was all the more perilous, with the "Devil's Elbow" providing opportunities to use all their skills. The vessel seen here is probably the *Juliet* or her nearly identical sister ship the *Romeo*, both of the Delta Transit Company. (Little Traverse Historical Society Collections.)

THE VILLAGE OF ALANSON. Located on the Crooked River just before Crooked Lake, Alanson was incorporated as a village in 1905. Alanson's first settlers arrived in about 1875. It was originally known as Hinman but was renamed in honor of Grand Rapids and Indiana Railroad president Alanson Howard in 1882 when the railroad first came into town. Crooked River lies just behind the row of buildings. (Doug Dailey.)

THE *TOPINABEE* AT ALANSON. The steamer *Topinabee* is seen here as it plies through the Crooked River on its way toward Burt Lake and eventually to the Hotel Topinabee on Mullett Lake. The voyage between Alanson and Topinabee began at 8:40 a.m. and arrived in Topinabee at noon for lunch; passengers were back in Alanson by 5:15 p.m. (Inland Water Route Historical Society.)

ALANSON RAILROAD DEPOT. The Grand Rapids and Indiana Railroad arrived in 1882 and built this depot, which is still standing today. As was common for Inland Route communities, many travelers began their journey by disembarking at the train station. Four regularly scheduled passenger trains passed through town every day each way, not including express and freight trains. (Doug Dailey.)

Downtown Alanson, c. 1895. This incredible view of downtown Alanson shows the bustling little downtown along Burr Avenue (U.S. 31.) From left to right is Klein's Dry Goods store, Walter W. Fairbairn Hardware (established 1892), Tom Hurst's general store, a saloon, and Thomas and Margaret Hurst's residence. Thomas Hurst is credited with opening the first store in Alanson around 1885; he later moved to the corner of Burr and River Streets before building the structure seen here (center). Fairbairn eventually bought out Hurst and occupied the entire building. W. W. Fairbairn and Sons remains in business to this day in the same building, now a registered Michigan State Historic Site. (W. W. Fairbairn and Sons.)

CROOKED RIVER BOAT, 1909. Measuring 17 feet long with a maximum capacity of six people and top speed of seven miles per hour, boats such as this were once a common sight along the Crooked River at Alanson for fishing or for a simple excursion. The image was taken from the dock at Alanson, probably from the same dock where Inland Route vessels docked as well. (Inland Water Route Historical Society.)

CROOKED RIVER IN WINTER. Taken from nearly the same place but decades later, little has apparently changed in the river at Alanson. Gasoline is still sold from the same shed, which advertises the price of 13¢ per gallon. Winter always put a halt to Inland Route traffic, but cut timber would occasionally be hauled across the frozen lakes. Ice fishing was also a popular way to pass the long winter days. (Inland Water Route Historical Society.)

No. 9. School House, Alanson, Mich.

THE ALANSON SCHOOL, C. 1912. The school building seen here was the second school built within the village. The foundation was laid in 1893, and it was a two-room schoolhouse when finished. Subsequent additions, however, increased its size considerably; the second story was added in 1900, and in 1910 a front addition was completed. Another two-story addition was completed in 1932 with a basement dug out for use as a gymnasium. Originally the school only had eight grades, and it was not until 1918 that a full four-year high school was in place. Due to consolidation with rural districts, the Alanson School was renamed Littlefield Township School in 1927. A modern, one-story brick school replaced this structure in 1957. On March 19, 1964, the old school was completely destroyed by fire. The insurance money was used to add a gymnasium/ auditorium onto the new school. (Doug Dailey.)

ALANSON SHINGLE MILL. Plenty of cedar trees grew up near the Alanson Shingle Mill, seen at the center of this c. 1890 image. The mill had a pond nearby where cut logs could be kept. This pond, called the Devil's Hole, was crystal clear, deceptively deep, and strange green colors could supposedly be seen emanating from its depths. The shingle mill burned in 1918. (Inland Water Route Historical Society.)

ALANSON WOODENWARE COMPANY. One of the most famous industries in Alanson's history is the Woodenware Company, which was regarded for manufacturing wooden bowls. Operating from 1890 to 1910, the factory produced bowls made of hardwood, including bird's-eye maple. Bowls in their earliest stage of production can be seen in this photograph. With a decreasing supply of hardwood, the mill was eventually sold and moved to Munising in the Upper Peninsula. (Inland Water Route Historical Society.)

PONSHEWAING ON CROOKED LAKE. Exiting the Crooked River into Crooked Lake, travelers along the Inland Route would have first met the tiny hamlet of Ponshewaing. Novacious M. Kellam, a store owner from Alanson, built a house here in 1897, which was enlarged into a hotel two years later. The establishment was situated back from the lake but still overlooked it; this image is taken from the front of the hotel, with an Inland Route steamer in the background. Initially Kellam wanted to name the hotel the New Klondike after the gold rush. But he then met a local Native American who told him that the area's name was Pon-she-wa-ing, or "the winter home." He then changed the meaning to "the summer home" and gave this title to his hotel. While working up the ground in front of the hotel, arrowheads were occasionally dug up, confirming the area's importance as a Native American site. (Inland Water Route Historical Society.)

PONSHEWAING, OR THE SUMMER HOME. The Summer Home grew to a hotel as a result of visitors disembarking from the train and seeking a place to stay at Kellam's home. The grounds included a trout pond, dock at the lake, boathouse, and an adjacent farm as well. The Summer Home received guests in the summer, but the Kellams lived there year-round. (Inland Water Route Historical Society.)

SUMMER HOME BOATHOUSE. The Summer Home was famous for its fishing. From this boathouse, a gasoline-powered launch made its way through the lake while towing up to six rowboats for a day out on the lake; they would be released as requested in either Crooked Lake or adjoining Pickerel Lake. In the late afternoon, the launch would return to pick up the rowboats and tow them back to the Summer Home. (Inland Water Route Historical Society.)

INTERIOR OF THE SUMMER HOME. Used both by vacationers and locals for fishing, the Summer Home at Ponshewaing always provided good meals, with many of the ingredients grown on-site. The dining room, seen below, was located in the east end of the hotel and the kitchen on the north end, with a total of 20 rooms on both the first and second stories. Also located on the property were farm buildings, storage sheds, and a woodworking shop. The Summer Home differed from other places along the Inland Route because it was not just a hotel, but truly a home as well. It was destroyed by fire in August 1955. (Both Inland Water Route Historical Society.)

VILLAGE AND DOCK AT ODEN. Though Conway lies farther west, Oden was considered by most to be the beginning of the Inland Route. Steamers departed from here and the "dummy trains" that ran from Petoskey had their terminus here (though they later went as far as Alanson). Passengers disembarked from the train at the station shown above and boarded an Inland Route boat at the Magnus Dock seen below. The c. 1902 promotional booklet *Where to Spend the Summer: Michigan Resorts on Little Traverse Bay* described that the community and its "picturesque scenery and quiet pleasures commend it to many who shun the more popular resorts." Smaller though it was, Oden still provided many of the comforts vacationers desired. (Both Clarke Historical Library.)

MAGNUS DOCK AND BOATHOUSE, C. 1912. In 1910, Joseph Magnus, promoter of the Oden Boat and Golf Club, built the boathouse and elaborate arched bridge seen here. Just to the left of the boathouse the stern of the *Tourist II* can be seen, and the ship at center is probably the *Rambler II*. (Clarke Historical Library.)

STEAMER ODEN, 1898. Many places along the Inland Route also had vessels named after them, from the *City of Cheboygan* to the *Argonaut Belle* to the *Topinabee*. Oden was no exception, as this image of the *Oden* shows. White woodwork and red plush cushions made her one of the most beautiful boats on the Inland Route. She was sold in 1910 and went to River Rouge in Detroit (see page 57). (Inland Water Route Historical Society.)

THE VILLAGE OF ODEN. Oden probably got its name from William Oden Hughart, president of the Grand Rapids and Indiana Railroad from 1874 to 1894. It was primarily a resort community, though there were some year-round residents, as there are today. In addition to homes, cottages, and hotels, an early promotional booklet of the era noted that boats were also available to rent for pursuing "fish of the finest varieties, and these in great abundance" on Crooked and Pickerel Lakes. (Clarke Historical Library.)

THE ODEN HOUSE. Little is known about the Oden House, though this photograph shows that the small community's post office is located inside the hotel. Many post offices of this era were located inside some other building, be it a store or a hotel. It is probable that this hotel later became the Atherton Inn, which burned in 1903. (Inland Water Route Historical Society.)

CROOKED LAKE AT ODEN. Crooked Lake had a reputation for its beauty as well as its fishing, making it the perfect place to stroll about the shores. An 1884 account in *The Traverse Region* declared, "I cannot begin to do this lovely lakelet justice; suffice it to say that we found it beautifully located in the forest primeval . . . a very gem in a silver lining." (Clarke Historical Library.)

SPEEDBOAT *PEGASUS*. Boat racing has long been popular on the Inland Route. From races in Mullett Lake hosted by the Topinabee Yacht Club to those once popular in Crooked Lake, racing is part of the route's heritage. Seen here is the *Pegasus* of Detroit at the races held in Oden on August 28, 1915. Today the Top-O-Michigan outboard races are still held on the Inland Route. (Clarke Historical Library.)

Rowden. House. Oden. Mich.,

THE RAWDON HOUSE (ODEN HOTEL). The Oden Hotel, later called the Rawdon, was probably the most elaborate and luxurious hotel on the Inland Route. Built in 1895 by Atherton Furlong, the Oden Hotel was designed to look like one of the steamships that meandered through the Inland Route. It had water on three sides so that boats could pull right up to the hotel and dock. Located just south of the railroad station, it even had its own power plant for electricity and to heat water for thermal baths on the lowest level. A stained-glass skylight allowed colored light to filter through the building, with each floor having an opening in the middle and an interior balcony. Rooms on the second floor were named after American cities, and named after countries on the third, while the top floor was mostly open. Furlong was unable to make the hotel a financial success, so he sold it to J. D. Rawdon, who renamed it the Rawdon House. (Clarke Historical Library.)

BOATHOUSE AT THE RAWDON. After the hotel was purchased by Rawdon, he filled in the water along the sides, while also concentrating on making the rear accessible by boats, especially Inland Route vessels. The boaters seen here are likely heading out into Crooked and Pickerel Lakes for a day of fishing; they also probably spent the night in one of the rooms on the bottom floor, as these were reserved for people who wanted to get up early and go fishing and thus not disturb the other guests. Each of these rooms on the lower level was named after a species of fish. (Both Inland Water Route Historical Society.)

COTTAGES NEAR ODEN. As the popularity of Oden and Crooked Lake increased, a number of cottages popped up along its shores, as these images show. The Westerman Cottage (below) is perhaps typical of those that dotted the lakeshore. Built in 1905 by Charles and Lucy Westerman, the lot cost its original owners $175. A small creek ran alongside the property and Westerman built a footbridge across it, with young birch trees providing a decorative railing. Many cottages of this type, large and small, still line the north side of Crooked Lake between Oden and Conway. (Both Clarke Historical Library.)

THE FOOTBRIDGE AT ODEN. Years later, a descendent of Charles and Lucy Westerman described the footbridge in Oden, "Grandfather had the creek dredged out and lined with railroad ties and kept his fishing boat up underneath the bridge. It was always needing rebuilding and repairs. My father built the last bridge in 1938. When it rotted out we did away with the bridge." (Clarke Historical Library.)

ODEN POST OFFICE, C. 1930. Just as with everywhere else along the Inland Route, change came to Oden via the motorized carriage. While hardly a bustling town, Oden continued to care for motorists passing through as they rumbled along the area's roads and the increasingly important U.S. 31. The sign for the Oden Post Office at left advertises not just the post office, but candy and ice cream as well. (Clarke Historical Library.)

STATE FISH HATCHERY, c. 1921. The State Fish Hatchery at Oden opened in 1921, with the building seen here completed in 1920. It operated until 2002, when a new complex was built, which is today one of the most advanced hatcheries anywhere. The old hatchery building was converted to a Great Lakes Watershed interpretation area, with the goal of increasing awareness of Michigan's fisheries; the new hatchery, rearing trout and salmon, lies just a quarter mile away. In decades past, state employees in charge of stocking fish traveled the state in special railroad cars complete with sleeping quarters and kitchens. One of these re-created and refurbished cars is available for viewing today on the site. Then as now, Michigan—and especially the Inland Route—is known for its fine fishing. One of the main draws of the Inland Route, in addition to relaxation and recreation, has always been fishing for sport or pleasure. (Little Traverse Regional Historical Society Collections.)

CONWAY BOARDWALK. Just west of Oden was the village of Conway—the final stop on the Inland Route. Conway was originally called Crooked Lake, but the name was changed to Dodge's Landing after W. E. Dodge donated land for a school and church. When Dodge's son Conway died in 1882 at the age of 11, the village was renamed yet again. Following the development of the Grand Rapids and Indiana Railroad, a post office was established in the same year. The boardwalk pictured here ran from the railroad station to the shores of Crooked Lake. A sawmill owned by Jim, John, and Arthur McFarlane operated here from 1870 until 1907, one of the first industrial establishments in the area. (Inland Water Route Historical Society.)

THE INLAND HOUSE. The Inland House was built in 1879 by Merritt Blackmer. The original structure had but five rooms; David Hastings purchased the hotel in 1908, added two more stories, and renamed it the Conway Inn. It was sold six years later to Homer Trask, who returned it to its original name. Though it has changed through the years, the modern Inland House still caters to visitors to the area. (Inland Water Route Historical Society.)

HASTINGS HEIGHTS HOTEL. Located on a hill just overlooking the village of Conway, the Hastings Heights Hotel was completed in the late 1880s. It was originally called the Lake Home Hotel and featured magnificent views as well as a golf course. It was away from any city life yet within a close walking distance to the railroad and post office. The hotel burned in 1919 and was replaced by the Sawkala Boys Camp, which operated until 1931. (Inland Water Route Historical Society.)

THE HIAWATHA HOTEL. The McFarlanes' sister, Mollie Matthews, opened the hotel seen here in 1900 to cater to summer guests of the area. Area hotels such as this provided a peaceful place to stay along the lake if visitors wanted to avoid the hustle and bustle of nearby Petoskey. The Hiawatha is still in business today. (Inland Water Route Historical Society.)

END OF THE INLAND ROUTE. Conway marks the last settlement on the Inland Route voyage. From either here or Oden, travelers would board a train and make their way to Petoskey. This image of Crooked Lake shows what is very near the westernmost point on the Inland Route. The large ships of old having been replaced, and fishing vessels now visit the dock. (Inland Water Route Historical Society.)

THE "DUMMY TRAIN." A complete Inland Route voyage usually meant getting off the train and boarding the dummy train into Petoskey. It gained the name because it usually consisted of a small "donkey" locomotive, tender, and just one or two passenger cars traveling back and forth. It ran exclusively between Petoskey and Oden, with several stops along the way; service was later extended to Alanson. The dummy train between Crooked Lake and Petoskey made its inaugural trip in 1878. The railroad, which ran on wooden tracks, was built by H. O. Rose and named the Bay View and Crooked Lake Railroad. Not known for comfort, the BV&CL was often unbecomingly referred to by locals as the "Busted Valise and Clothes Line." Whatever one chose to call the line, it was effectual in both bringing visitors to and from Petoskey, as well as supplying the community with its mail. (Little Traverse Regional History Society Collections.)

Grand Rapids and Indiana Train. When the Grand Rapids and Indiana Railroad came to the area in 1882, it took over the services provided by the BV&CR and installed steel rails; the railroad also did away with the donkey engines and moved to larger locomotives, such as the one seen here. The passenger cars had benches made of wood and were arranged back to back. The seats were painted gray, and the floor and exterior were red. One former traveler reminisced, "A stray cinder sometimes lodged in an eye; this usually happened when the engine was running backward and was next to [behind] the passenger coach." In an era where the condition of roads was intolerable and walking or stagecoach not a good option, the dummy trains provided the needed link between Petoskey and its surrounding communities and Crooked Lake. A voyage on the Inland Route could then go completely through much of Northern Michigan. (Little Traverse Regional History Society Collections.)

The Song of Hiawatha. Before arriving in Petoskey, those riding on excursion trains could stop to see a dramatization of Henry Wadsworth Longfellow's epic poem *Hiawatha*, which was based on the legends of the Ojibwa Indians. It was presented daily from the end of June to the end of August (Sundays excepted) from 1905 until about 1916 at Round Lake, a small lake just west of Crooked Lake (and not on the Inland Route). The performers were local Native Americans, and the stage was the lake itself, with the natural surroundings providing all the scenery necessary. Play performances were organized and heavily promoted by the Grand Rapids and Indiana Railroad as one of the many attractions to see in the Petoskey area. Visitors disembarked from the train at the Round Lake (Wayagamug) station before spending the day bathing or fishing on the lake; visitors might purchase items crafted by local Native Americans at kiosks set up underneath bleachers built on the shore for viewing the pageant. Later in the day, the celebrated play would begin. (Inland Water Route Historical Society.)

Departure of the Warriors.

THE "DEPARTURE OF THE WARRIORS." The *Song of Hiawatha* included a scene in which an actor jumped off a cliff into the lake. The director, L. O. Armstrong, was first based out of Ontario. The play traveled to Chicago, New York, Philadelphia, and Detroit, and enjoyed a European tour in 1905. The production ran out of money and rights were transferred to the GR&I. (Inland Water Route Historical Society.)

"CHIEF" IGNATIUS PETOSKEY. The city of Petoskey gets its name from Ignatius Petoskey (Pe-to-se-ga), though originally the settlement was known as Bear River. Petoskey was first settled on the south shore of Little Traverse Bay around 1840. He and his sons eventually owned much of the land upon which the city now stands. Hiram O. Rose set up a temporary store in Petoskey's house in 1873; he called him "Chief" out of respect, and the name stuck. (Author's collection.)

NATIVE AMERICAN WOMEN AT PETOSKEY, C. 1890. The area around Petoskey, like all of Northern Michigan, owes much of its history to the influence of Native Americans. Its location inside Little Traverse Bay no doubt provided a place of refuge, with the proximity of the Inland Route providing the opportunity to travel further inland. (Little Traverse Regional Historical Society Collections.)

BAY VIEW DEPOTS. In January 1876, the Michigan Campground Association of the Methodist Episcopal Church selected a site near Petoskey for the establishment of a summer campground for revival meetings and religious and intellectual instruction. The Grand Rapids and Indiana Railroad liked the idea as well, and that year it extended its line from Petoskey to the site, dubbed Bay View. The resulting campground soon became a small settlement onto its own, with beautiful Victorian cottages, railroad stations, a post office, an auditorium, and other community buildings. It remains a religious association to this day and is on the National Register of Historic Places. Seen here are the Bay View railroad station (above) and the Reed Street Station (below). (Both Little Traverse Regional Historical Society Collections.)

BAY VIEW HOUSE, C. 1882. The Bay View House was one of several hotels in the Bay View area. The first hotel in Bay View, it was built about 1876 and was later enlarged in 1882. The influx of summer visitors meeting friends or coming for religious instruction meant that adequate accommodation was necessary. Owing to the fact that Bay View was supposed to be a restful and relaxing destination, the hotels there spared no expense in catering to their guests. The Bay View House overlooked Little Traverse Bay and was close to the railroad depot, the steamboat dock jetting into the bay, and was immediately adjacent to the campus and community grounds of the association. Other hotels in Bay View included the Howard House, the Roselawn, and the Kenilworth Hotel. Today two hotels remain: the Terrace Inn and Stafford's Bay View Inn. (Little Traverse Regional Historical Society Collections.)

THE BEAR RIVER. Sites along the Inland Route such as Cheboygan and Indian River were settled at least partly because of the rivers that run through them. While Petoskey is not directly on the Inland Route, its proximity to it and the presence of a river puts it in nearly the same category as an Inland Route community. From the time it was first surveyed in 1841, a note was made that the Bear River would one day make "the very finest of mill sites." From Andrew Porter's first gristmill, later bought by Hiram O. Rose, to the Shaw-McMillan Lumber Company, the McManus Mill, and the Petoskey Fibre Paper Company, the Bear River has been the nucleus upon which Petoskey prospered. It too suffered with the decline of the lumber industry in the early 20th century, but it retained some of its industry while continuing to be a destination for vacationers and resort visitors. Petoskey was known as Bear River until the name of the community was changed in 1873 to honor "Chief" Ignatius Petoskey. (Little Traverse Regional Historical Society Collections.)

THE DOCK AT PETOSKEY. Travelers arriving at Petoskey frequently did so on vessels operated by the Michigan Transportation Company; Hannah, Lay, and Company; Detroit and Cleveland Navigation Company; and the Chicago, Duluth, and Georgian Bay Transit Company. Upon disembarking, visitors would stroll about the midway, where they could purchase a variety of items from local vendors. Here the *City of Charlevoix* can be seen at the dock in Little Traverse Bay (above). Those making their way off the boat would have seen Petoskey as it gracefully rises above the bay (below). An observation tower is visible, as well as the Perry Hotel and Clifton House. (Both Little Traverse Regional Historical Society Collections.)

EARLY VIEW OF PETOSKEY. In 1882, the author of a brief summary of Petoskey observed, "It is difficult to realize, as one sits on the veranda of his modern hotel, enjoying his after-dinner smoke, and looks over the busy, thriving village . . . that but a few brief years ago only the canoe [of the Indian] cleft the lucid waters of Little Traverse Bay." Indeed, Petoskey had been settled rapidly. When the Grand Rapids and Indiana Railroad first came to the little village in 1874, there was very little activity. It was the railroad, however, that made the growth of the area possible. Eight years after the railroad came to town, the population had swelled from a few dozen hardy souls to 2,500. Industry was an important motivating factor, as was the temperate climate and opportunities for rest and relaxation. (Little Traverse Regional Historical Society Collections.)

Petoskey Overlooking the Bay. This image of Petoskey shows its immediate proximity to Little Traverse Bay. The area was first made available for purchase from the federal government in 1874 and 1875, and settlement blossomed afterwards with the help of the railroad. While the railroad was important in bringing people at all times of the year, the docks seen here in the bay allowed summer vacationers to sail in on one of the great steamers that once plied the Great Lakes. Petoskey's location was not lost on its early settlers, nor is it lost on those who visit or live there today. The 1882 *Historical Sketch of the Village of Petoskey* states, "This pure, soft, resinous air is a sovereign balm for many ills that flesh is heir to. . . . Candid doctors are saying to their patients every day, 'I can do nothing more for you; go to Petoskey, and try the air.'" The air may have attracted some settlers, but like most northern communities, it was primarily driven by the prospect of commerce. (Little Traverse Regional Historical Society Collections.)

GRAND RAPIDS AND INDIANA SUBURBAN STATION. It was from this station that the dummy trains coming back and forth from the end of the Inland Route at Alanson, Oden, or Conway had their terminus. After boarding the train at any of these locations, passengers reached Petoskey and their Inland Route journey had truly come to an end. Within just a few short miles, those voyagers would have gone from the peace of the Inland Route to the hustle and bustle of a real urban city (at least by Northern Michigan standards). Along the way, guests would have passed through Bay View, most of them probably unaware that it was partially because of the resort community that the railroad existed there at all. The GR&I loaned the Bay View Association's founding fathers some $3,000 so that they could purchase the property upon which the community is now situated. Banking on the fact that Bay View would be a success, their intuition was rewarded by the increased traffic that followed not just to Bay View, but to the entire area as well. (Little Traverse Regional Historical Society Collections.)

RAILROAD TRACKS AT THE GR&I STATION. The area around the Grand Rapids and Indiana station was a welcoming one, even if it was a busy place. A park surrounded either side of the tracks, and hotels nearby welcomed weary travelers for business or pleasure. Amenities could be found immediately adjacent to the park as well—from bakeries and confectioneries to the ubiquitous saloons found in most any good boomtown. (Little Traverse Regional Historical Society Collections.)

CHICAGO AND WEST MICHIGAN PASSENGER STATION. Challenging the GR&I's hegemony in the area, the Chicago and West Michigan Railroad extended its line into Petoskey in 1882 and built the ornate train station seen here. It was used until the early 1960s before falling into disrepair and being scheduled for demolition. Concerned citizens saved the structure, however, and today it houses the Little Traverse Regional Historical Society Museum. (Little Traverse Regional Historical Society Collections.)

THE ARLINGTON, C. 1896. The Arlington Hotel was the largest and grandest hotel in Petoskey. Constructed in 1882 at a cost of $60,000, the Arlington had three stories and a unique basement, visible in this *c.* 1896 image. This basement held a dance hall and two billiard halls. The first floor contained the office and reception room, complete with velvet carpet and a piano, as well as dining rooms. An advertisement from 1882 described it best, "It adjoins the beautiful 'Marquette Park,' and commands the most charming view of Little Traverse Bay. The house is provided with gas and all the modern improvements. It is built with especial reference to the accommodation and comfort of pleasure seekers who spend their summers in Northern Michigan. H. O. Rose and Company, proprietors." Visitors apparently not only agreed but spread the word as well; the year after the Arlington opened, an additional 60 rooms were added. (Little Traverse Regional Historical Society Collections.)

THE NEW ARLINGTON. So successful was the Arlington that it was enlarged yet again with the construction of an additional story, while the exterior was renovated and an elevator installed. A 12-foot veranda was replaced with a 24-foot one, and steam heat was put in place as well. The hotel was equipped with a music hall, bar, bowling alley, casino, and even a barber. The Arlington's new 800-guest capacity briefly eclipsed that of the Grand Hotel on Mackinac Island; thus, the Arlington, now renamed the New Arlington, was for much of its life the world's second-largest summer hotel. The parties and balls held at the New Arlington were the social events much of Petoskey's high society revolved around. The New Arlington continued to be the most important hotel in Petoskey until it was completely destroyed by fire in June 1915. (Little Traverse Regional Historical Society Collections.)

THE CUSHMAN HOUSE.
Prior to the construction of the Arlington, the Cushman House was the finest hotel in Petoskey. Built in 1874, it was in constant competition with its rival across the street, the Occidental Hotel (formerly the Rose House). Both hotels attempted to outdo the other with the constant improvement of landscapes, expansions, or the addition of some other new accoutrements. The Cushman was larger, but what really set it apart was the porch that extended above the entrance in a half circle, which was added in 1899. An annex operated in connection to the Cushman burned in 1928, but the hotel itself was a victim not of fire, but of the Great Depression. It was torn down in the early 1930s. (Both Little Traverse Regional Historical Society Collections.)

THE HOTEL PERRY. The Perry Hotel, one of the first brick buildings in Petoskey, was constructed in 1899 by Norman J. Perry, a dentist who left his practice after a patient died in his office after extraction of multiple teeth. The hotel provided first-class accommodations for up to 150 guests, affording beautiful views over Little Traverse Bay. In 1926, a four-story addition doubled the capacity. By 1961, it was purchased by John R. Davis and renamed the Perry-Davis. Today it is known as the Perry once again, and it retains the elegance of the Gilded Age in which it was built. (Author's collection.)

DOWNTOWN AT MITCHELL STREET, C. 1945. In the heart of downtown Petoskey, Mitchell Street has been the site of the city's bustling business district from its earliest days. Hotels, dry goods, grocers, furniture and millenary stores, banks, saloons, and liveries all once graced the downtown area. The J. C. Penny Company, still in business today, can be seen at right in the center of this image. (Author's collection.)

HERMAN WELLING. Herman Welling and his family came to Petoskey in 1892 and sold clothing and finishing goods for the next 74 years. He operated two stores, one on Mitchell Street and the other on East Lake Street, before combining both at the Mitchell Street store. Despite setbacks such as a devastating fire and even bankruptcy, he is remembered as one of many successful Petoskey businessmen. (Little Traverse Regional Historical Society Collections.)

PETOSKEY PORTLAND CEMENT COMPANY. A longtime fixture along the lake just south of Petoskey was the Petoskey Portland Cement Company. Originally founded as the Petoskey Crushed Stone Company in 1907, it reorganized 10 years later to produce cement. Located near deposits of calcium carbonate and shale, a 1919 advertisement claimed, "No cement plant is more favorably located for the manufacture of cement, and with two railroads on its property and a dock on the lake front [*sic*] its transportation facilities are better than any other company of its kind." By 1952, the plant employed 375 people. In 1955, it was sold to the Penn Dixie Corporation. Following a bankruptcy in 1979, it was closed in 1980. The plant sat abandoned and was a major source of pollution in the area until 1994, when demolition and environmental cleanup work began. A barrier was removed between Little Traverse Bay and Bay Harbor, forming what is now Bay Harbor Lake. Today the site of the old cement plant is the center of the community of Bay Harbor, a four-season luxury resort community. (Little Traverse Regional Historical Society Collections.)

INGLESIDE INN, DOUGLAS LAKE. The story of the Inland Route would not be complete if other waterfront, inland locations in the area weren't mentioned. They are important because, though they were not on the route per se, they still offered vacationers to the area the opportunity to explore the area on the water. Douglas Lake, located just north of Burt Lake, was home to two such places for recreation and relaxation: Douglas Lake Resort and the Ingleside Inn. Located on the northwest portion of the lake, the Ingleside Inn was operated by Lambert J. Wilson and offered rates of $2.50 per day in 1920. A small community sprang up around the hotel, complete with its own post office. (Both author's collection.)

DOUGLAS LAKE HOTEL. The "New Douglas Lake Hotel" seen here is really not so new at all. The hotel was originally known as Bryant's Hotel and had a dock that could be used to venture to nearby Pell's Island, which jets out into the lake; a post office was located on the site as well. Today this building is home to Douglas Lake Bar and Steakhouse, a somewhat hidden jewel of fine dining nestled between the thick woods and cottages nearby. Douglas Lake is also home to the University of Michigan Biological Station, with a campus of around 150 buildings. Formed in 1909, its mission is to foster "education and research in field biology and related environmental sciences," and "to produce biologically knowledgeable graduates who are prepared to understand, deal with and solve environmental problems." It is home to a 24,000-square-foot laboratory, lecture hall, and extensive library. (Author's collection.)

BLACK RIVER AND ALVERNO. Just south of Cheboygan, the river splits; while the Cheboygan River continues on to Mullett Lake, the Black River connects to Black Lake on the east side of the county. While there was little activity on Black Lake (probably owing to the fact it was not directly on the Inland Route), the farming community of Alverno sprouted up roughly halfway between Cheboygan and Black Lake. Once named Sova after many of the area's settlers, it received a post office in 1899. The Black River Dam is also located in Alverno and at one time was used to generate electricity. (Both Doug Dailey.)

MICHIGAN STATE FERRIES

MICHIGAN STATE FERRIES. Two communities on the Inland Route had the honor of being the namesakes for two of the ferries that once connected the Lower Peninsula of Michigan with the Upper. Operated by the State of Michigan for 34 years, the state ferries carried 12 million vehicles and 34 million people across the Straits of Mackinac. Prior to the completion of the Mackinac Bridge in 1957, the only way to cross the straits was via ferry. The State of Michigan operated eight different automobile ferries, including the *City of Petoskey* and the *City of Cheboygan*, seen on this postcard. When the Mackinac Bridge opened on November 1, 1957, all automobile ferry service to the Upper Peninsula stopped. The *City of Petoskey* was eventually scrapped, while the *City of Cheboygan* was cut down and reduced to a barge used for storing potatoes. (Author's collection.)

The Inland Route. When considering the history of Northern Michigan, few things rival the Inland Route. It has been used for hundreds, if not thousands of years, and it will likely remain an important fixture in the region's future. From the Native American travel and encampments of old, to the glorious hotels, towns, and villages that popped up in its heyday, to its continued use for recreation, the Inland Route will remain a vital artery in the north. White settlers learned from the Native Americans' use of the route and built many of their communities along it, and the wisdom of those who came before is evident in the utilization of the route to this very day. While the great vessels that once made their way along the route, such as the *Topinabee* (pictured), have steamed their way into history, their role in its past makes up but one chapter in the diverse story that is the Inland Route. (Inland Water Route Historical Society.)

SELECTED BIBLIOGRAPHY

Aloha and Aloah: Now and Then. Cheboygan, MI: The Aloha Historical Society, 2000, 2001.

Banwell, Yolanda. *Alanson, Our Town: 1882–1982.* Northern Lakes Lithographers, 1982.

Browne, Arline M. *In the Wake of the* Topinabee: *Cherished Memories of Lakeside Cottages.* Lancaster, CA: Hubbard Map Service, 1967.

Byron, M. Christine and Thomas R. Wilson. *Vintage Views of the Charlevoix-Petoskey Region.* Ann Arbor, MI: The University of Michigan Press, 2005.

Cheboygan, Up-to-Date. Cheboygan, MI: Cheboygan Democrat, 1898.

Fennimore, Keith J. *The Heritage of Bay View.* Grand Rapids, MI: William B. Eerdmans Publishing Company, 1975.

Friday, Matthew J. *Among the Sturdy Pioneers: The Birth of the Cheboygan Area as a Lumbering Community, 1778–1935.* Victoria, BC, Canada: Trafford Publishing, 2006.

Guth, Fred E. and Eleanore Cave. *A Bit About Mullet Lake Village.* St. Louis: Fred E. and Eleanore Cave Guth, 1975.

Hill, Mark. "The Steamer Topinabee and the Inland Water Route." www.iwrhs.com/history.htm

Historical Sketch of the Village of Petoskey. Petoskey, MI: City Record Book and Job Printing House, 1882.

Jarvis, Nancy H., ed. *Historical Glimpses: Petoskey.* Petoskey, MI: Little Traverse Printing, 1986.

Liebner, Mary Davis. *All Aboard: The Boat's Leaving.* Cheboygan, MI: 2008.

Sager, Robert C. *The Pageant of Tuscarora.* Burt Lake, MI: Northern Lakes Litho, 1975.

Traverse Region, Historical and Descriptive, Illustrated, The. Chicago: H. R. Page and Company, 1884.

Ware, W. H., Rev. *The Centennial History of Cheboygan County and Village.* Cheboygan, MI: Northern Tribune Printing, 1876.

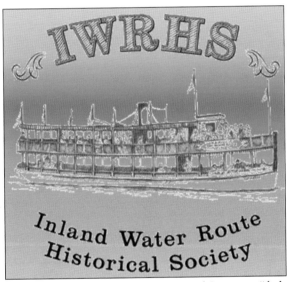

Founded in August 2004, the Inland Water Route Historical Society is "dedicated to maintaining and preserving the history of the Inland Water Route in Northern Michigan." The society seeks to disseminate knowledge of the Inland Route through publications, presentations, and its museum in Alanson. It also seeks to preserve the memories, stories, images, and artifacts of the route.

www.arcadiapublishing.com

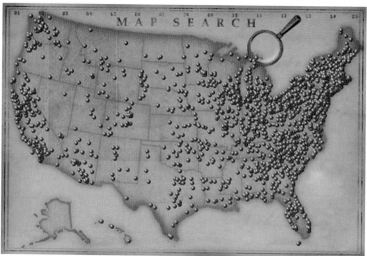

Discover books about the town where you grew up, the cities where your friends and families live, the town where your parents met, or even that retirement spot you've been dreaming about. Our Web site provides history lovers with exclusive deals, advanced notification about new titles, e-mail alerts of author events, and much more.

Find Your Place in History.